THE FABULOUS LOST & FOUND

AND THE LITTLE SWEDISH MOUSE

WRITTEN BY MARK PALLIS
ILLUSTRATED BY PETER BAYNTON

D1737966

NEU WESTEND
— PRESS —

Thanks Tomas - MP

For Max and Maya - PB

THE FABULOUS LOST & FOUND AND THE LITTLE SWEDISH MOUSE

First Printing, 2020
ISBN: 978-1-913595-06-7
NeuWestendPress.com

THE FABULOUS LOST & FOUND

AND THE LITTLE SWEDISH MOUSE

WRITTEN BY MARK PALLIS
ILLUSTRATED BY PETER BAYNTON

NEU WESTEND
— PRESS —

In the middle of the big city is a tiny
yellow building. If anyone loses anything, this is
where it ends up.

It is called the Lost and Found.

Mr and Mrs Frog keep everything safe, hoping that someday every lost watch and bag and phone and toy and shoe and cheesegrater will find its owner again.

But the shop is very small. And there are so many lost things. It is all quite a squeeze, but still, it's fabulous.

One sunny day, a little mouse walked in.

"Welcome," said Mrs Frog. "What have you lost?"

"Jag har tappat min hatt," said the mouse.

Mr and Mrs Frog could not speak Swedish. They had no idea what the little mouse was saying.

What shall we do? they wondered.

Maybe she's lost an umbrella. Everyone loses an umbrella at least twice, thought Mr Frog.

"Have you lost this?" asked Mr Frog.

"Ett paraply? Nej," replied the mouse.

Then Mrs Frog remembered something that had been handed in a few months ago...

"Is this yours?" Mrs Frog asked, holding up a chunk of cheese.

"Ost? Nej, det stinker!" said the mouse.

"Time to put that cheese in the bin dear," said Mr Frog.

"Maybe the word 'hatt' means coat," said Mr Frog.

"Now where did I put that nice
yellow one?"

"Got it!" said Mr Frog.

"En kappa? Nej. Jag har tappat min hatt," said the mouse.

She was starting to feel a bit frustrated.

"We need to keep trying," said Mrs Frog.

Inte en halsduk.

Inte ett par byxor.

Inte en tröja.

Inte ett par solglasögon.

Inte ett par skor.

"Jag har tappat min hatt," said the mouse.

Inte två cyklar.

Inte en dator.

Inte tre böcker.

Inte fyra bananer.

Inte fem nycklar.

It was no good. A fat wet tear rolled
down the mouse's cheek.

"How about a nice cup of tea?" asked Mrs Frog kindly.

"Jag älskar te. Tack," replied the mouse. They sat together, sipping their tea and all feeling a bit sad.

Suddenly, the mouse realised she
could try pointing.

She pointed at her head.
"Hatt," she said.

"I've got it!" exclaimed
Mrs Frog, leaping up.

"A wig. Of course!" said Mrs Frog.

"Nej, det är inte en peruk,"
said the mouse.

Inte röd.

Inte blond.

Inte brun.

Inte mångfärgad.

Inte grön.

"What about this?" asked Mr Frog, pulling back a curtain.

"Hatt!" exclaimed the mouse.

"Ah, so 'hatt' means hat. I should have realised. Silly me!" Mr Frog laughed.

För lång.

För liten.

För trång.

För stor.

"One hat left," said
Mrs Frog, reaching all
the way to the back of the
cupboard.

"It couldn't be this
old thing, could it?"

"Min hatt!

Jag hittade min hatt.

Tack så mycket," said the mouse.

And just like that, the mouse found her hat.

"Hej då," she said, as she skipped away.
"Hej då," replied Mr and Mrs Frog.

"I wonder who will come tomorrow?" said Mr Frog.
Mrs Frog put her arm around him.

"I don't know," she replied, giving him a squeeze,
"but whoever it is, we'll do our best to help."

LEARNING TO LOVE LANGUAGES

An additional language opens a child's mind, broadens their horizons and enriches their emotional life. Research has shown that the time between a child's birth and their sixth or seventh birthday is a "golden period" when they are most receptive to new languages. This is because they have an in-built ability to distinguish the sounds they hear and make sense of them. The Story-powered Language Learning Method taps into these natural abilities.

HOW THE STORY-POWERED LANGUAGE LEARNING METHOD WORKS

We create an emotionally engaging and funny story for children and adults to enjoy together, just like any other picture book. Studies show that social interaction, like enjoying a book together, is critical in language learning.

Through the story, we introduce a relatable character who speaks only in the new language. This helps build empathy and a positive attitude towards people who speak different languages. These are both important aspects in laying the foundations for lasting language acquisition in a child's life.

As the story progresses, the child naturally works with the characters to discover the meanings of a wide range of fun new words. Strategic use of humour ensures that this subconscious learning is rewarded with laughter; the child feels good and the first seeds of a lifelong love of languages are sown.

For more information and free downloads visit www.neuwestendpress.com

jag har tappat min hatt	I've lost my hat
ett paraply	an umbrella
ost	cheese
det stinker	it stinks
en kappa	a coat
en halsduk	a scarf
byxor	trousers
solglasögon	sunglasses
tröja	sweater
skor	shoes
en	one
två	two
tre	three
fyra	four
fem	five
dator	computer
bok	book
nyckel	key
cyklar	bicycles
bananer	bananas
Jag älskar te	I love tea
tack	thank you
peruk	wig
röd	red
blond	blond
brun	brown

grön	green
mångfärgad	multicoloured
nej	no
min hatt	my hat
för lång	too tall
för stor	too big
för liten	too small
för trång	too tight
jag hittade min hatt	I've found my hat
tack så mycket	thank you very much
hej då	goodbye

Made in the USA
Las Vegas, NV
05 April 2022